Published by Gwen Cheryl Lyn Sarandrea, M.A., San Rafael, CA.

Other books by Gwen Sarandrea are available at:
Amazon.com, BN.com, GwenSarandrea.com & MontageMirage.com

Montage Mirage Photo Tapestries, How To Create Photo Art From Your Heart

Frank Lloyd Wright's Marin County Civic Center Commemorating 50 Years

Poster of Frank Lloyd Wright's Marin County Civic Center

The Healing House, The Gift of Dad's Final Years

GwenSarandrea.com
MontageMirage.com
Google.com/+GwenSarandrea

Frank Lloyd Wright's
Marin County Civic Center
Commemorating 50 years

Gwen Cheryl Lyn Sarandrea

GwenSarandrea.com
MontageMirage.com
Google.com/+GwenSarandrea

The Civic Center, designed at the end of Wright's career, is a National Historic Monument and World Heritage Site. Enjoy 66 color photos of the interior and exterior of the Civic Center plus the exterior of the Veterans Memorial Auditorium, Marin Exhibition Hall, Fire Dept., Post Office and Lagoon Park.

Available at Amazon.com & BN.com.

Commemorating 50 years

MARIN COUNTY CIVIC CENTER

SAN RAFAEL, CA

Designed by Frank Lloyd Wright

Montage Mirage Photo Tapestry™ by Gwen Sarandrea
www.MontageMirage.com
© 2013 Gwen Sarandrea

Frank Lloyd Wright Montage Mirage Photo Tapestry **poster** of the Marin County Civic Center in San Rafael, CA., commemorating 50 years available for purchase at **GwenSarandrea.com & MontageMirage.com.**

I took over 700 photos of the whole complex designed by Frank Lloyd Wright at the end of his career which includes the Civic Center, Memorial Auditorium, Exhibiton Hall, Post Office, Fire Station, Lagoon with fountains, circular pools and Lagoon Park then, trimmed the best down to their essence and Montaged Miraged them. The Civic Center has a full atrium down the center of the two long arms planted with trees, shrubs and flowers under a glass dome. **The poster is 18" x 24" on coated paper.**

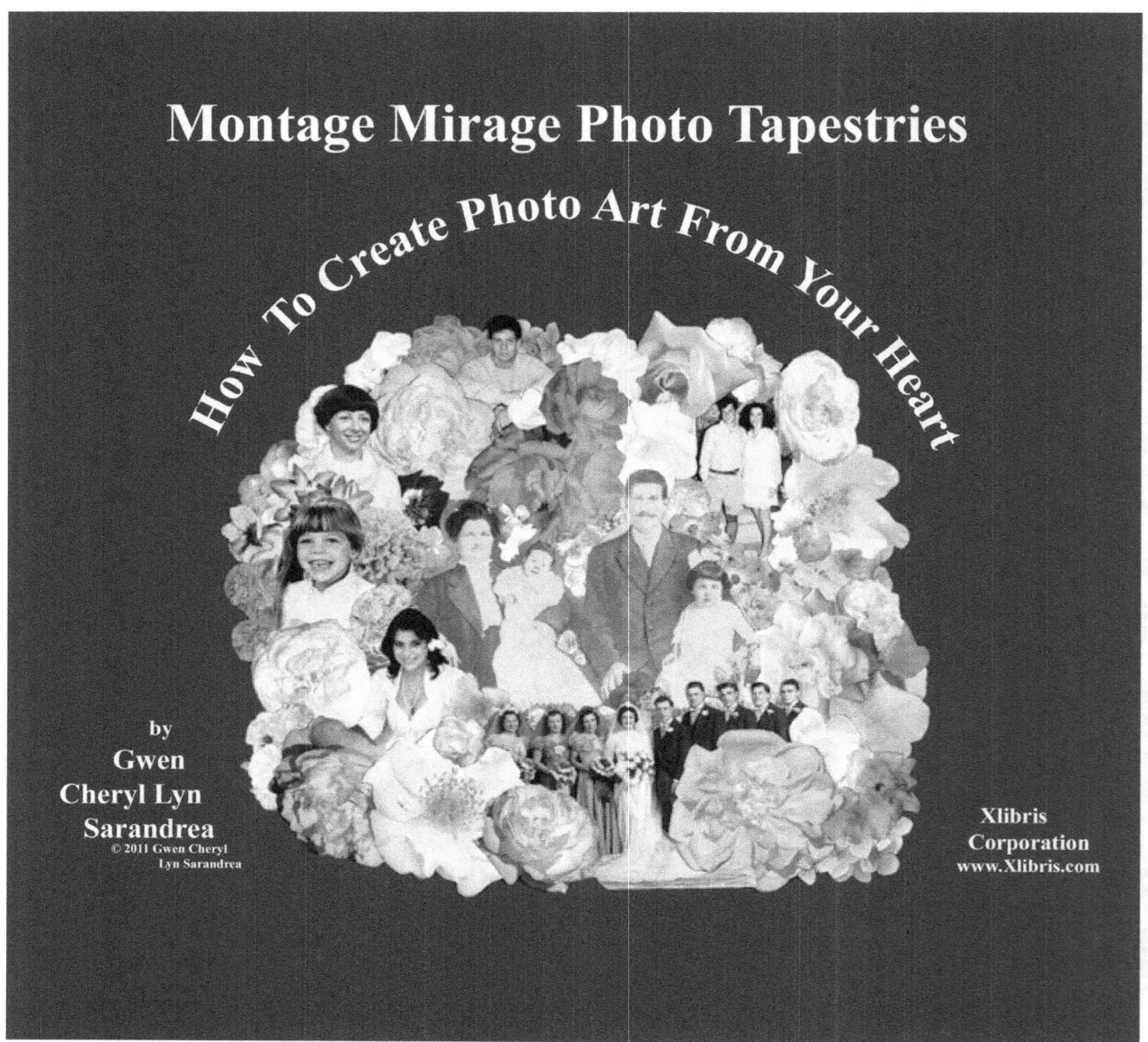

Montage Mirage Photo Tapestries, How To Create Photo Art From Your Heart available at MontageMirage.com, Amazon.com, BN.com

Montage Mirage is completely original and creates one-of-a-kind pieces. The process is easy, fun and stimulates creativity. Follow one of the basic layouts - substituting your own photos - and it will be customized for you. Always color copy your precious photos onto photo paper first, then work with the copies so you have nothing to lose. You now have the ability to chronicle your own family's events. Inspiration permeates this book and empowers you with the knowledge and tools needed to create your own personalized photo tapestries.

The Healing House
The Gift of Dad's Final Years

How Living With Dad Transformed Us Both

Gwen Cheryl Lyn Sarandrea, M.A.

GwenSarandrea.com

In 1994, Gwen invited her 80-year-old widowed father to move from PA. to CA. to live with her. They bought a 1914 home and remodeled it together. The Healing House, The Gift of Dad's Final Years describes their story and how this home became a metaphor for the transformation of their individual lives and their relationship.

Five years later, Gwen shared his hospice home care with her sister, Carole. She found that the ultimate gift of her father's final years came after his death when Gwen saw a vision of him alive and vital on the Other Side.

Available on Amazon.com & BN.com

Counseling Case Study

Joseph's tall, slender physique houses a man with a dry wit who takes responsibility seriously. He applies his careful, methodical thinking equally to family, profession and creative writing projects.

The fifth son of well-educated, immigrant parents, Joseph was his mother's favorite. He was schooled in the Catholic tradition though he later rejected a personal, traditional God.

Andrea, Joseph's quiet, well-mannered wife, had just earned an M.A. in education. Their relationship is close, supportive, loving and has deepened over two decades of marriage. They have parented three sons.

When Joseph came to the Counseling Center, he was in his late thirties. He recalled a significant emotional crisis after college graduation. Having excelled scholastically in college, he entered a Ph.D. program to study psychology in direct opposition to his father who wanted him to follow in his footsteps as an engineer. Joseph said, "I thought I could survive my father's wrath – after all, I had a four year scholarship and stipend. I was financially independent."

However, three months into the program he dropped out, describing his experience in the following way: "The University was a highly pressured place and my sense of self-esteem was bound up in my success of being a top student. So, when I got into a very competitive program where there were a lot of bright people – with half of them dropping out or flunking out before the end of the year – it was sheer terror… I started to psychosymaticize… and I fled… I just fled. It was after that that I was really down on myself for not staying and working it out. I started to visualize – to have a big daydream. In fantastic imagery, I would see myself hanging from a tree. It was crazy… I had no serious intentions of committing suicide, but went through a real depression. For a long period of time I had deep feelings of self-hate… I came out of there really screwed up."

Joseph didn't know what he was going to do. He applied to graduate schools in everything from philosophy to theology to engineering (which was the last thing he wanted to do). Then he accepted another psychology scholarship, but again quit. Joseph went into crisis intervention counseling for three months. All the time, he was fighting his father's pressure to become an engineer. "So there was a struggle going on and I was living at home… there must have been an awful lot of resentment at my father."

Finally succumbing to parental demands, Joseph entered engineering college. It came easy to him and he graduated first in his class. "Then the problem with my father was resolved. I had done what he wanted me to do."

Six years later, Joseph was diagnosed with leukemia, the result he now believes of "feelings and images of self-destruction." His wife was pregnant and he thought he was going to die. After receiving the best available treatment, the diseased remised, but Joseph feared it would recur. Two years later he said, "it did – in accordance with my expectations… the dropping out of school is what I see as the cause of my becoming ill."*

---

*Many studies show that stress and repressed negative feelings, such as resentment and hate, may be primary causes of cancer.

Counseling Case Study

In Getting Well Again, Carl Simonton, M.D., states: "Chronic stress results in a suppression of the immune system, which in turn creates increased susceptibility to illness - and especially cancer."*

"… and because cancer patients often have unresolved resentments, and other emotional ties to the past (as we have seen, perceived abandonment or rejection by one or both parents may be an antecedent to the development of cancer), helping our patients learn to release the past is often essential to helping them get well. Processes that help people release resentment, express negative feelings, and forgive past wrongs (whether real or imagined) may well be a major part of the preventive medicine of the future."**

(Fear of abandonment was a major issue dealt with in several of Joseph's eleven sessions).

Body, feelings and mind are inter-related and inter-dependent aspects of the personality. A dysfunction in one necessarily affects the others. In his book, Psycosynthesis,*** the Italian psychiatric pioneer, Roberto Assagioli, formulates the inherent relationship of the physical, emotional and mental faculties of man into empirical psychological laws.

Law 1 states that, "Images or mental pictures or ideas tend to produce the physical conditions and the external acts that correspond to them."

His father's open disapproval, together with the stress of a highly competitive academic program had caused Joseph to psychosymaticize. Think of what possible long-term effects the repressed emotional trauma experienced upon returning home to father defeated, coupled with subsequent years of working in the family profession, together with dwelling on self-destructive images like hanging from a tree could have had on Joseph's physical health.

In the third law, Assagioli states: "Ideas and images tend to awaken emotions and feelings that correspond to them." When a person thinks dismal thoughts, his feelings begin to resonate with them and his disposition begins to match those thoughts.

When Joseph was "down on himself" he became depressed and had corresponding feelings of "selfhate."

Assagioli's fourth law states that "Emotions and impressions tend to awaken and intensify ideas and images that correspond to or are associated with them." Hence, a negative feedback loop is created and sustained. The resulting combined heaviness or depression of the mind and feelings weigh the body down reducing its energy and affecting it adversely.

---

*Simonton, O. Carl, M.D., Stephanie Matthews-Simonton, James Creighton, J.P. Tarcher, Getting Well Again. New York; St. Martin's Press, 1978, pp. 51

**Ibid, p. 164

***Assagioli, Roberto, M.D., Psychosynthesis: a Manual of Principles and Techniques. Middlesex, England: Esalen, Penguin Books Ltd.

Counseling Case Study

On those days when one is feeling depressed, it seems that even getting out of bed takes too much energy. Consider the long term effects of chronic thoughts of self-destruction and feelings of self-hate such as those Joseph reported – on his physical state. Is it possible that Joseph's physical body came to reflect the self-hate being experienced and energized in his mind and feelings?

During the course of his illness, Joseph "received a revelation" that changed his life. He wrote, "Sitting in my study in my home, I suddenly realized many things: that my doctors could not cure me, but I could cure myself; that I was responsible for the disease and for the cure; that fear and worry were responsible for the disease coming back. I cried, as I am crying now, as I realized these things; I realized I was ambivalent about living; I opted to live, not die; I declared myself cured; resolved never to worry again. Having arrived at my destination - cure - I would now find the means to get there, the means of survival. During the next few years I found those means; among them were meditation, visualizations, Edgar Cayce medical readings and practices, acupuncture, change of diet, exercise, affirmations, psychic healing, bibliotherapy, as well as radiation and chemotherapy."

Joseph came to see his search for physical wholeness as a search for spiritual wholeness, as well. He acquired an intense interest in spiritual and psychic phenomena such as para-normal and self-healing, meditation, energy systems of the body and energy transfers, and various spiritual paths.

As an undergraduate, a course in philosophical psychology, exploring the nature of man, had excited and challenged him. He now became even more intensely interested in discovering man's true nature because he "had certain experiences of a transpersonal nature which indicate to me that man is a more complex and perhaps qualitatively different person than the being described by orthodox Western philosophy and religion… I have come to believe that man is potentially divine, i.e. some aspect of him always was, always will be."

He described some of the "evidence" which "contradicts the materialist premise and led me to radically alter my belief in what man is." After completing an intensive meditation course, "I was able to go into a deep state of physical and mental relaxation and yet remain conscious. On one level, I did not think this feat possible or even desirable. On another, I knew that it was because I did it. I was given names of people I did not know – people in various parts of the country. The names were supplied not by the instructors, but by the other students. While in 'alpha', I 'saw' these people, could describe them and some of their physical ailments with uncanny accuracy. I left the course, wondering who I was, who man was."

After several out-of-body experiences, Joseph wrote, "These experiences indicate to me the possibility of the viability of consciousness separated from a physical body."

These and several other extraordinary experiences "kindled my interest in consciousness, spirituality and transpersonal states."

Joseph decided to quit his highly successful engineering career to probe deeper into his own and mankind's nature and to return to his earlier pursuit of psychology, after affecting his cure through the previously described means. This decision brought intense feelings to consciousness, however, and before he could bring himself to tell his father, he underwent ten weeks of Gestalt therapy to deal with fear and repressed anger toward him. Then Joseph "steeled" himself to break the news to his elderly father at Sunday dinner. To his surprise, Dad was not only interested in the program, but supportive of it. He had become religious in his old age, and Joseph spoke to him of the spiritual aspect of his quest for the knowledge of man and of the strong service impulse to help people which impelled him to study counseling.

So, after moving his family to California, Joseph enrolled in an M.A. program in Transpersonal Psychology.

The first of the three Psychosynthesis guides who worked with him over the next year and a half reviewed the material Joseph presented.

From it, she was able to deduce several things. He was strongly identified with his excellent, well trained mind (mentally-identified). Deeply repressed negative feelings were markedly influencing his thinking, attitudes and behavior, causing conflicts and rationalizations in important areas. The most striking was Joseph's life long struggle to assert and maintain his own individuality and life purpose in the face of his father's rigid expectations and the dread that God had tried to kill him through terminal illness.

When the guide considered which feelings would be most likely to cause the chronic anxiety he described, repressed fear and anger seemed most probable.

Was his deep need for approval from father/authority figures a reaction to Joseph's unconscious fear or his father's? His inability to persist in two separate psych programs against his father's wishes and his inability to copy with less than top student status while in those programs – when academic excellence was a major means of obtaining father's approval – supports this hypothesis.

The guide knew that channeled expression and release of repressed anger usually results in increased strength and personal power. An example of this was Joseph's successful confrontation with his father concerning his change of career plans after working through some of this anger in Gestalt therapy.

Often, patterns that we experience in relation to father are projected onto other male authority figures and on a higher level, onto one's concept of God.*

---

*When a client's issue of the reality of the existence of God becomes important and seems to become relevant in the client's personality behavior, then clearly it needs to be evoked in counseling like everything else. The first thing to find out is what the client means by God – there are many different interpretations. There will be some kind of mental construct based on the client's belief. Unless clients have a very strong direct experience with spiritual realities, almost inevitably we find some conceptual construct that may not be in any way related to realiy.So, it is important that this construct be brought to light and examined for its merits or lack of merit and dealt with appropriately. That is just as important for clients who have a strong belief in a spiritual reality as it is for clients that have a strong aversion – either can be significant and limiting. You are not trying to take it completely away but are clearing these misconceptions, illusions and distortions. This then, opens the road for the client to be free to explore deeper into the actuality of reality than he was before – if he wishes to do so. Of course, that's something that (continued next page)

Counseling Case Study

During the course of counseling, Joseph repeatedly dealt with the incessant fear that God had eliberately struck him with leukemia in order to kill him and would complete the task if He now realized that Joseph had survived. He submitted the following writing:

"When I heard about the disease, I begged God for life, begged and prayed with a passion I didn't know I had. And then a terrible anger took hold of me. And I began to have a daydream, a fantasy that went as follows: 'Somewhere up on a hill lives the deity. The hill is always covered in darkness. And there are trees, or rather shrubs, behind which a deity can hide. But if a man set out, with determination and defiance and armed with an ax, he has but a chance to meet the deity. He must go in the night and climb the hill. His feet must dig into the earth to brace himself from the wind coming off the hill. And then, when he reaches the shrubs, he must go behind each one until the deity is found. He must challenge the deity to a fair fight. And with the ax, he must slay the deity. Then, the wind will still and the man will be able to walk from the hill, bleeding slightly from the scratch wounds, but free. The man will be free."

"When I wrote this fantasy down about 10 years ago, I did not realize what it meant. It was in symbol, the prototype of my myth: I wanted to become free (healthy, whole, immortal, eternal). And in order to become free, I had to kill God. But these things do not happen at once. God does not die easily. I continued to be angry at Him, continued to fear Him. What if He finds me? Will He try to finish me off? Since He might do that, I had better stay out of His way. Keep a low profile. That became my strategy. Stay low. Image: In a war, bullets winging over my head. I'm glued to the ground."

This is a symbolic representation of Joseph's on-going struggle with father/God, a theme that dramatically colors his entire life. The guide saw how this life/death competition with God was blocking communication with Joseph's inner source of guidance by keeping him constantly poised against outside danger.

In accordance with these feelings, Joseph attempted to hide his existence from God (keeping a low profile) by becoming egoless in the Eastern philosophical sense. He attempted giving up his whole personality on the premise that if he had no ego, God couldn't kill him. He rejected all ambition – the desire to be a published author, to be famous or successful – in order to hide. This presented him with a very interesting double bind, because he had used ambition as an effective means of gaining father's approval. He reported the absence of male authority figures' approval (father, et al) as causing him much tension and anxiety throughout his life.

Before considering the long term direction she would choose for the work, the guide also noted the positive motivation and strengths of character that would assist Joseph in his growth. His deep sense of ethics and moral responsibility were evident, not only in his personal life but also in his professional career.

---

can be recommended by the guide if that seems to be relevant to the client's existential situation. The guide needs to be very careful not to impose or even suggest his own beliefs or world view but rather, try to give the client as much freedom and space for the client to find out on his own.

Counseling Case Study

He expressed an ardent desire for self-understanding, a firm belief in the power of the mind, spoke of his goal of expressing Superconscious qualities – like love, harmony and joy in his daily life, and was willing to put hard work behind his desire to help people through the study of Transpersonal psychology.

Not only had he developed his imagination through writing, but he had also developed various qualities of will, i.e., discipline, persistence, one-pointedness and determination.

The guide saw that what Joseph lacked most was access to and control over his feelings. In order to integrate his personality (to have his mind, body and feelings working together for the same purpose) , she decided to focus the work on first getting to his repressed feelings and helping him experience them as much as he was able. Over time, she would help him cathart negative emotions that were blocking his growth and teach him to take responsibility for them. She set this as her long term direction.

The guide hypothesized that the fear and anger would be most accessible and looked for signs of them in his initial sessions. However, she would be ready to work with whatever feelings were most present for him at the time. (Often, it is easier to help a mentally-identified client with heavily repressed feelings to experience his positive feelings first, as a way to familiarize him with experiencing emotions in a nonthreatening way).

Because imagination is a powerful way to bypass a controlling mind and access repressed feelings, the guide chose to use mental imagery in the first session. His mental faculty is his superior function and it seemed to be repressing his feelings – which is precisely where the work needed to focus. Working with his creative imagination would allow repressed unconscious material (i.e., feelings) to emerge in symbolic form.

The guide can then work toward resolution of the personality conflict by working with the symbols themselves, acknowledging and expressing the feelings related to them. Afterwards, the guide can help the client interpret the symbology, see the pattern inherent in it and its application to his current life situation. By understanding what needed to happen in order to resolve the symbolic conflict, the client can then apply the same principle to the corresponding dysfunctional pattern in his life. This "grounding phase" of the counseling process is very important because if the client does not bring what he learned from his session into his daily life, the changes that occur may not be lasting.

From the beginning, Joseph demonstrated great facility with imagery. (Some clients need to be taught to visualize. Images need not be clear and distinct. Often the client gets only a dim sense of an image which is sufficient to continue working. In time, the ability to visualize improves).

The guide directed Joseph to close his eyes and imagine himself in a meadow using as many senses as possible. He was then asked to see a mountain with a path leading up to it. (A mountain usually symbolizes a person's goals and Joseph's guide wanted to bring out and help change Joseph's old, ineffectual patterns of dealing with life goals).

As soon as he saw the mountain, Joseph magically flew to the top. He was using his imagination to bypass what proved to be a difficult journey for him. The guide directed him to fly back down and begin the ascent on foot. (This is the only way that she would be able to see what hinders him and help him overcome it.)

As he climbed, he soon became blocked by an impassible ledge that was part way up a steep, perpendicular wall. (This represented a block to achieving life goals). When the guide evoked Joseph's feelings about the ledge, he was scared. Then a green clown appeared above him on the ledge. The guide had Joseph ask the clown what he was doing there and he replied that he wanted to help Joseph climb over the rocky ledge. (The clown is a subpersonality that uses humor to elevate and was ready and willing to help Joseph overcome his fear). Joseph was afraid to trust the clown and the contraption that he built to carry Joseph up. If it didn't work, Joseph feared that he would fall off the high cliff and die.

In order to work out this important trust issue, the guide had Joseph imagine that he is the clown and Joseph became him. As the green clown, he experiences no malice toward Joseph but, in fact, feels love for him. He tells Joseph that his struggle to prove he's worthy is unnecessary.

After experiencing the clown's goodwill, Joseph became himself again and made a choice to trust and he continued. (It is important to evoke the client's will when he needs to go beyond his fear by having him make a clear choice to go on). Once at the top, he was told to describe it and to imagine a bright sun shining down on him. (The sun is a symbol for the Higher Self radiating Superconscious energy. This technique helps facilitate the inflow of Superconscious qualities which replace negative energy that the client has released that (as was true in Joseph's case) acts as a future ideal model which points to the client's next step and therefore helps set the direction of future work.)

Superconscious qualities that Joseph experienced when the sun streamed down on him were clarity, light-heartedness, peace and serenity. It is interesting to note that, at the time, his heavily repressed feelings were clouding his mind, weighing him down with a sense of burden and anxiety, and were causing conflict and stress in his personality. The positive-opposite qualities experienced at the top would eventually replace the negative emotions released over time through the work.

For homework, Joseph was to visualize himself daily in his meditation at the top of the mountain and allow the qualities of clarity, peace, light-heartedness and serenity to come into him. He also saw that he could dialogue with his Wise Old Man (who in the daydream had resembled Groucho Marx!) whenever he had flashes of fear. The guide asked him to begin to look for practical ways that he could bring these qualities into his everyday life.

Also, as part of his outside work, the guide assigned various readings from Psychosynthesis & the Act of Will* and the Synthesis Journals** as a means to get his mind actively cooperating with his goal of selfrealization.

---

*Assagioli, Roberto, M.D., Psychosynthesis & the Act of Will. Middlesex, England: Esalen, Penguin Books Ltd.

**Synthesis Graduate School, San Francisco, CA.

Between sessions, Joseph did much work on his own, putting into practice both psychological theory and experiential learning from his own sessions. At home, he listened to each taped session, expanding his own sessions, expanding his own understanding of personality patterns, recording further insights and questions regarding dynamics for his guide. In addition, he supplied her with updates of significant process work that he did on his own. This outside session work is an important part of the grounding phase of Psychosynthesis and greatly helped to accelerate his growth.

During the next several sessions, the guide followed her direction by continuing to help Joseph experience his repressed feelings in order to begin releasing the blocked energy. She saw that anger was present below the surface and began to focus on it.

He began this session with a story about his wife having been away for several weeks in connection with her work. He had noticed that he was angry that she was gone. Then he thought about how ridiculous it was to be angry at her and began to rationalize away his feeling. The guide used this issue to bring him into relationship with his anger. The following partial transcript is an excellent example of releasing emotional energy with a strongly mentally-identified client through imagery as a first step toward eventual physical/emotional catharsis. It also illustrates a completely spontaneous transformation of anger into creative energy.

G. See if there are two parts there, one that thinks it's ridiculous and one that has the anger.

C. Yeah, I certainly can separate the part that says, "You're the one that's allowing this to happen, why are you blaming anyone but yourself – it's all in your psyche – you're the one that's at fault for causing this to happen. It has nothing to do with her." That's the rational voice. Then there's this other part that says, "I just feel like I'm being stepped over and I'm really angry about that. And all I wanna do is respond – to yell out and be angry and flail my arms. I don't care about ideology, causation or anything else."

G. Tell that to the reasonable part, "I don't care about…"

(Thus the guide promotes a dialogue between the two conflicting parts).

C. To the reasonable part – I don't care about all the theories, all the psychodynamics and everything else, I just care about I'm hurt and I'm angry and that's all there is to it!

I see an image of picking up a log and smashing the reasonable part over the head (laughs) and beating him into the ground.

G. Good. Stay with the image. Experience yourself doing that.

(Since Joseph usually expresses the "reasonable part" and represses the angry feelings, the guide ecourages him to allow his anger to vent itself within the imagery which is safe and nonthreatening to him or his wife. Through this technique, he'll understand his anger better in the future and learn that it is manageable so that he can begin to deal with it rather than denying it).

C. The reasonable part is getting smashed into the ground (laughter). I'm feeling good. The reasonable part is saying, "This is even more ridiculous!" as he's being smeared to the ground. He's shouting, "You're making a complete fool of yourself even imaging these things." And then, there's part of myself that's vicious and angry and has big teeth, and it's just involved in this orgy of destruction of smashing at this guy. Meanwhile, the rational part is being physically forced down into the ground.

(The client is still observing the two parts, so the guide directs him to imagine himself as the angry part, to experience the anger to facilitate catharsis).

G. Stay with the experience of being this part with the log. Be that part smashing the reasonable one. What do you experience in your body as you do that?

(Focusing the client on his bodily experience helps him get into the part. Describing his body sensations helps anchor the experience so that he can begin to identify as fully as possible with the emotion to be expressed).

C. I experience strength, aliveness, like the adrenalin is flowing. A kind of wholeness. I don't feel afraid – just the opposite of that. I don't feel that terrible fear feeling that I get sometimes or the anxious feeling. I'm in control. I feel good about that. The more I do, the more I enjoy it, too. It would be literally that type of orgy continuing it, then going beyond and I don't see satiation in sight.

G. Keep going … keep on beating it.

C. I see just keep on doing it and doing it and doing it, just there smashing and smashing and smashing!

G. Let your body go with that – do what it wants to do.

(Ideally, the guide would like Joseph to be able to begin to physically beat on the pillows provided for this purpose in order to fully release his pent-up anger as he experiences it. This is too big a step for him at this time, so she gently encourages whatever amount of bodily participation he can manage in order to deepen the experience as much as possible – like the clenching of fists).

C. It's smashing down, down, down. I'm standing, I'm smashing down, hitting, hitting, hitting. As I hit down more, I seem to get lighter. It's very freeing, getting stuff out that's in there.

(He began to rhythmically pound the coach with his fist is a rather controlled way).

G. Good. Keep doing that. Let your body participate and do what it wants to do. What's happening in the imagery? What are you doing?

C. I'm just experiencing the release of tension – a state of physical satisfaction. I no longer need the other part. I'm just standing by with the log – not physically attacking this other part anymore.

G. Stay with the experience of being the part. What do you want to do?

C. Now that he's cleaned up, I would like to go out of the room where this guy is and take on the whole world (laughs)… instead of having a little log which was all that was needed to take on the part of me that felt that I was ridiculous, I would need something bigger – like a big stick – and then go out and wreak havoc on other parts that are getting me angry.

G. See yourself doing that.

C. I see myself going out and I have this stick that's 15 feet long, 20 feet long and I'm swinging it and knocking down buildings and knocking down lamp posts and poles and anything in my way. I'm just knocking it down… swinging this thing… walking on the street smashing things.

(The guide keeps the energy moving within the imagery).

G. Just keep going – releasing that energy. Go where you want to go – see what happens.

C. I'm shouting, I am pissed. I am pissed. I am angry, I'm mad … I don't know where I'm going with it. I'm just swinging and flailing and knocking things down… there's a whole city block that's just knocked out. All buildings are just rubble on the ground and then I can just stand over it with my stick and surrey the ruins.

G. How do you experience yourself now?

C. In my mind I see this figure with the stick standing there just looking at a whole city block that's down on the ground.

(The client has slipped back into the observer's position. The guide brings him back to being the angry image).

G. Be that figure – look out through his eyes.

C. OK. It's almost like I'm a big, lean, mean animal and I'm just looking out – to see if there's anything else that needs to be wiped out.

G. How do you feel?

C. I'm still angry, still a little bit. I'm intent on finding anything else that needs to be taken care of.

G. Like what?

C. Whatever else that seems to need to be taken down – seems decrepit or old or no longer functional, no longer useful – everything that's in the way, I just want to take it down, smash it down and get all the rubble out of the way… get it cleaned up. I see myself cleaning it up now – with brooms and piles and sticking it on wheelbarrows and trucks and carting it away to clean out the whole area … I have a whole operation of people and it's all kind of unfolding. It's happening with these other people building.

G. What are they building?

C. Other things in the area that I had taken everything down in this whole city block and carted off all the rubble. And the image that I'm just following – rather than creating – is I'm standing there watching as these other people, who are under my direction, are building – a building made out of steel and out of glass.

(The old structure that he destroyed represented obsolete personality patterns that were once necessary (like childhood defense mechanisms) but which were now outmoded and held him back. As he expressed the anger, symbolically he dismantled those out dated patterns. The angry energy released naturally and spontaneously transformed into power – which he then used to create a totally new and different pattern that more closely conformed to his unique needs and was aligned with the direction of his individual adult growth. This is an example of transformation of negative energy that has been expressed into its positive opposite quality).

C. I'm in control of this operation now – all the weak parts are out.

G. Which parts are those?

C. I saw them as these bricks – these decrepit buildings – as the weak concrete old buildings. And that's what I was angry about – that weak part. Now, something that's going to take the place of the weakness.

G. What's going to take the place of it?

C. This whole new structure made out of steel and glass, that's going up very quickly. And they're building it and it's very tall.

G. What's the quality of the building?

(Here is an example of the importance of staying in touch with the client's experience. As Joseph described the building materials (concrete, steel and glass) the guide got the sense of something very sterile, cold and lifeless. When she asked for the quality of the building, the form was the same but he gave a very different picture than she had imagined).

C. Sun can get into any part of the building. And the steel is sunk deep, deep into the ground so that there's nothing that can shake it. And it's very high and it's also very aesthetically beautiful. It's made completely out of glass except for the steel beams which are in the corners and the cross beams. Even the floors are made out of glass – the roof is made out of glass – there's nothing hidden in this structure. You can look at any angle – from the top to the bottom – see in it and across and through it. People can walk in it – it's useful. It can be used. People inhabit all parts from bottom to top. It's 20-30 stories high. People are doing things in each room. They're busy, excited, cooperating.

(This image is quite different from "keeping a low profile" and hiding his existence from God so that he would not be destroyed. More work was required before Joseph could begin to actualize the ideal model that this new structure represented.

Joseph then described groups of people happily doing things in the various rooms. This could also be interpreted as his various subpersonalities cooperating with each other toward a more integrated personality.

The glass structure with sun streaming in everywhere is an example of the concrete mind illumined by the soul (represented by the sun) which is often a transitional stage when the abstract mind is coming in. His concrete mind is very, very powerful and the abstract mind is not as present and accessible to him yet).

As the sun shone in, Joseph went to the roof. The guide directed him to experience sun shining on him. He then saw himself taking a shower, washing himself, getting clean and feeling happy with his creation. (Washing is a symbol of purification). The guide asked what happened to the anger.

C. It got transformed into the building. It very quickly and naturally replaced that which had been torn down in anger – that energy that includes destruction and building – it's a power that can be directed to destroy or to build. I can feel it in my hands.

Even though we think of anger as being destructive, it can be channeled for useful purpose as a first step to elevate it and turn it into something that is more appropriate.* Often forces that turn out to be destructive – in a sense are energies that are misdirected. Expressing anger, from a different perspective can be a very useful thing to do at times – like channeling it to remove obstacles. Think about what's the most constructive thing you can do with it.

---

*Anger/rage can be lifted to indignation. Indignation is the result of seeing that something bad is being done to something good where there's a spiritual connotation for both, i.e., I'm outraged that this bad action is blocking this good action. It's not you – but what you're doing. Indignation sees you as good – doing something bad – when you know better. Or, I can be indignant at myself for having missed something good when I knew better (or even if I didn't).

Because we confuse indignation with anger, we often block it or tend to deal with it like anger. Indignation is a good and useful source of energy – leading to spiritual dignity (which is related to how you see yourself). It's good to have access to it. Build it so that the next time you see something, your indignation can turn it and make it stop.

For example, "From now on, I won't stand for that kind of stuff. I know that's not really what you want to do. I love you – you are a good person – but I am indignant that this is happening and I want it to stop."

Anger is often the result of frustrated desire – which comes from attachment to something and at the same time not having the power to do it. In his case, as his will develops more and more, one could normally expect situations in which his getting angry would decrease.

The guide brought Joseph back into relationship with his wife in imagery with the sense of creative power that he was still experiencing. He expressed love and support for her work and felt no threatened or angry feelings towards her. (Of course, anger will come back but his is now better equipped to deal with it and to transform it. If he chooses not to express it directly in the moment, he can use his vivid imagination to dissipate the energy and channel it for a useful purpose rather than repressing it).

As he reached out to support his wife's growth, he felt whole within himself. When he opened his eyes, the energy in his hands remained. He remarked, "I didn't think the stuff with my wife and my feelings had anything to do with anything." The guide inquired about what he saw now. "It's so connected to the rest of my life," was his answer, "by allowing the anger, I connected to the creative energy in back of it and they both come from the same place."

For homework, the guide instructed him to look for the patterns in his personality that correspond to the decrepit buildings in the imagery, that are old and no longer useful so that he can consciously begin to tear them down and replace them, thus creating space for the ideal model to emerge.

She also suggested that he connect to energy of that creative power and seek ways to use it in his daily life –making sure to separate the energy from the forms.

In the following session, Joseph was aware of internal conflict. One part said, "Watch out – God, the giant/destroyer, might knock it down." (The glass building). Another part said, "That's completely nuts! I realize that God as the giant/destroyer is a projection of my own power – afraid not that it can destroy me, but I can destroy myself."

The guide had a choice of working directly with the part that feared God as a giant/destroyer or of going after a misconception of God to get real experience of spiritual dimension. She decided to investigate the latter and asked him to tell her more about that part. It said, "Whatever is out there doesn't engage in the petty activity of destroying people – it's at least benign – maybe beneficial or helpful. I'm really the giant/destroyer."

G. Stay with whatever is out there may be beneficial.

(The guide decided to pursue this part, bring it to his consciousness awareness and build it in order to neutralize the giant/destroyer image.)

C. Not in a personal sense of God – in the Judeo/Christian sense, but in some kind of Super consciousness of which we all partake and that I, too, partake of. I have a sense that's there in some form… I'm not really sure – some kind of pool – common source that we can tap into … our individual egos can be temporarily distracted or submerged so that we can cut through that and then, get into this other, deeper channel which flows through it all.

Counseling Case Study

When asked how he knew this, Joseph recalled his experience of doing psychic health diagnostics with its accompanying sense of "knowing." He said, "I think I was experiencing at least one layer, one level of this channel… a new level of being that went beyond the materialistic level."

As the guide penetrated deeper, Joseph recalled the awe and reverence that he had felt then and also remembered experiencing the power of that connection when healing himself. This was the beginning of his spiritual quest. "Faced with the prospect of dying – I wanted to experience divinity here – whatever that was – to the extent it was here… I wanted to experience my own immortality…there was a conflict because I don't believe in a personal God."

As the guide probed deeper, Joseph recalled a dramatic experience of "shedding everything but my "I consciousness." She asked him to describe it in detail and brought out his feelings as he did.

While ill with leukemia, he experienced a "terrible need to be alone." He drove to the country, rented a cabin with a canoe and paddled into the middle of a deserted lake around dusk. He began thinking that if he fell into the water, no one would ever know. "Suddenly images came up out of me of myself as something… son, father, husband, brother… in different postures – all started to peel off. With that, a sense that I was descending a spiral… I was terrified –afraid that I'd disappear… every possible thing I could think of peeled off me… until all images were exhausted, until nothing was left except a prayer that I breathed and it was "I AM" and I remember crying… tears of being tremendously appreciative that there was this indestructible part of me."

("… the 'I' – which is the core of the whole personality - is a spark of pure being, without qualities in the ordinary sense. But though it has no qualities, it has functions, and its two main functions are consciousness and will. Through 'self-identification' – or identification as the 'I' – we gain the greatest freedom to use that consciousness and will – or more exactly, we re-own what are in fact our consciousness and our will. When we use our consciousness while remaining identified as the 'I', we take the attitude of observer. Similarly, when we use our will, we take the attitude of director."

"Experiences of liberation or 'disidentification' from a specific, restrictive state of consciousness, are not uncommon. Yet they often go unrecognized. Many people have had similar experiences though they are usually less dramatic and so less easy to understand for what they are. Because of this lack of understanding, many miss the opportunity of applying them and making… lasting changes in their lives.*

The guide often evokes the client's "I" in session to allow him to recognize the experience, help him to see how he got there so he can get back and so that he can begin to use the "I" as the unifying center of his personality. "As the 'I', we not only have experience of personal identity and individuality, we can also be most objectively aware of our psychological life and our interactions in the world and can therefore guide our actions and development with the greatest effectiveness."**

---

*Identity & Personal Freedom by Betsy Carter-Haar Synthesis, The realization for the Self, P.57

**Ibid. P. 63

Whenever a client has a peak experience, it is very important to have the client describe it in detail and re-experience it again in slow motion. That is, the guide can slow it down and help the client get the full understanding of the experience so that he can bring important aspects into his daily life.)

The guide continued to deepen Joseph's experience by having him describe the "indestructible part".

    C. Being without being anything – without being a particular type of person, no traits there – not even a body – just "I AM". It's peaceful, no fear, no good or bad.

(Joseph then recalled listening to the waves but the guide brought him back to his inner experience of "I AM".)

    G. Allow the sound of the waves to recede. What else are you aware of?

    C. At some time I have to go back to the everyday life.

    G. That's true – but see what else you're aware of in the moment… a sense of "I AM"…what else?

The guide was holding a world view that included this experience in a larger one – a more expansive reality that he could become aware of.)

    C. The world's stopped… (long pause) it seems to just bottom out… the experience of "I AM" – it may be that opens up, too, and there's something underneath.

    G. What's the something underneath?

    C. I don't know. I am in a deep level, but there's still a form there. Maybe that form, too breaks up.

    G. What's your experience as you contemplate that?

    C. Mystified… because I don't know what that would be… I suppose it would be like an awakening.. it's a sense of knowing that I talked about before – a sense of certainty … I can't prove it but no one could argue with it either.

    G. Stay with that knowing… see if you want to move toward the experience of even this form, this "I AM" breaking open… toward whatever it is that's beyond even this pure, content less form.

(The guide saw an opportunity to expand the client's consciousness beyond his personality and "I" to a more realistic experience of the Spiritual dimension. By asking if he wanted to, she evoked his will to align it with the same direction she had chosen – which also helps to reduce potential resistance to moving beyond the form to the energy animating it – to the "source" that he sensed earlier.)

    C. Yes, I'd like to do that if I could.

Counseling Case Study

G. What do you experience with that wanting?

C. A little excitement, a little fear... a lightness and wonderment.

G. Stay with that. Just begin to move forward. Imagine yourself as that, "I AM" moving in whatever direction seems right to you. Whatever direction represents the "beyond" of this experience.

(The guide is totally trusting the process – that it will unfold naturally and individually.)

C. There's a wanting to let go of that – fall far from it, fall through space.

G. Good. Let yourself do that... (long pause) What do you experience?

C. Movement at tremendous velocity... any consciousness there is, is involved in this movement... and that there's no place, there's no form or receptacle for this I AM. Still something there.

G. What is the something that's still there?

C. There's focus, a consciousness that's moving – like cells of consciousness. They're concentrated – as fast as they move, they'll still in the space – that particular place in space... and I have this image that even these cells must separate and diffuse and disappear.

G. Follow that process of the diffusion & disappearance of those cells.

C. Go off into the cosmos – disappearing, blending...

G. (Long pause) What are you aware of now?

C. Of being no place, being every place.

G. Are you still moving?

(The guide is checking on his experience so that she knows where he is.)

C. No... I'm like a blackness – goes everywhere.

G. Are you aware of anything in that blackness?

C. Nothing.

G. So, there's only blackness ... Stay with that and say what happens.

(Again, the guide is staying with the client's experience while holding the view that there is a source of light that he will reach if he goes through the blackness.)

C. Somehow I get a sense that my own boundaries extend as far as the boundaries of the blackness and I fill it.

G. Stay with that. See if you can become aware of what's beyond the boundaries of the blackness.

C. I can see the boundaries of the blackness falling away and then, lightness and I expand and fill that and that boundary falls away. It seems that can keep on happening and happening. It gets lighter as it happens.

G. Good. Stay with that experience of the boundaries falling away and the experience of the increasing light… as you continue, allow yourself to move toward the source of that light.

(The guide had Joseph move closer to the source of light until its intensity and radiance blinded him.)

G. What's happening now?

C. I'm trying to get into it… and seeing what that experience is that's stopping me. It has something to do with turning to that light and then becoming blind to other things.

G. What kind of things would you become blind to?

C. Anything that's dark.

G. How do you feel about that?

C. I'm trying to get used to what that means or what the notion of being blind means.

G. So there seems to be a choice between moving toward that, seeing that which might blind you to seeing something else. (Um Hum). So that you'll be able to see the light or see this other thing. (un huh). See if you can get a sense for what the other thing is – what is the dark that you wouldn't be able to see? Is there an image for that?

C. It's just dark like dirt or soil… white light is like a purifying light. The soil has to do with being of the earth. Once you're baptized or experienced of this white light, then you're no longer of the Earth.

G. How does that make you feel about those two things – to see that?

C. I'm being pulled both ways. I want both. I don't want to give up the earth – what's physical, what's concrete… and yet, I'm attracted to the light. Knowing that at some point you go into the light when you do give up the earth. Seeing that that's a transition that we take. Like saying, "OK, that's what happens." I wanted to get close enough to see that and know about it now… I wanna know what's ahead and then I can go back. I still want to be of the earth for now.

G. Good. Tell that to the light… to that point of light that's too intense to look into.

Counseling Case Study

(Here the guide began a dialogue with the light because Joseph was choosing not to go into the light. She hypothesized that it might be his fear that prevented his merging with the light and if it was right for him to go beyond his fear, the light would tell him that directly.

Clients can and do merge with the source of light during sessions and it is a very beautiful and profound experience.)*

C. I see your tremendous source of brilliance and power and it's something that I'm attracted to and know one day I'll be absorbed into this light. Yet, I know to do this, there's a complete giving up of the earth. But I don't want – at this time – to give up the earth. (The light asks me why?) Because I have much to do on earth yet. I have a lot to learn and I have to teach what I've learned and pass that on. I have children to father. I have to improve and leave the earth in a better way than I found it. I feel very strong, very definite about that. That I'm still attached to the earth, to my body, to experiencing life in this form. And if anything, I want to the extent that I can, to bring down into my body and into my life not only the memory of the light, actually a piece of it.

G. What does the light say?

C. It says that I can use as much of it as I can bear to use, tolerate. It doesn't limit the amount of what I can draw on but that I've limited that. It talks about opening up parts of me so that its light can get into those parts. It's opening up … I don't know if it's a physical body or another type of body… to let that light come in.

(The following intervention maintains direct dialogue between the client and the light while getting information from the light itself about how to help the opening.)

---

*Social scientists McCready & Greely conducted a research study on mystical experiences in which they interviewed 1400 persons chosen as a representative sample of the population of the United States. To a key question, "Have you ever felt as though you were close to a powerful spiritual force that seemed to lift you out of yourself?" as many as 35% replied, "yes." Of these, half also indicated that such experiences had occurred "several times" or "often."

A. Greely: The Sociology of the Paranormal: A Reconnaisance, Sage Publication, Beverly Hills, CA & London, 1975, pp. 58 & 65. This type of experience and expansion of the world view toward "the good, the true and the beautiful" – (Plato) – has very much a universal quality. It also has been commonly reported among people who have had near death experiences. "Particularly common (to many dying individuals) seem to be visions of a Being of Light which appears as a source of unearthly light, radiant and brilliant, yet showing certain personal characteristics such as love, warmth, compassion and a sense of humor…"

The Human Encounter with Death, by Stanislave Grof, M.D. and Joan Halifax, Ph.D., E.P. Dutton, New York, 1978, p. 155.

Descriptions of a "Being of Light" Life After Life by Raymond A. Moody, Jr., M.D. Bantam Book, 1976, New York, NY. pp. 58-64. "What is perhaps the most incredible common element in the accounts I have studied, and is certainly the element which has the most profound effect upon the individual, is the encounter with a very bright light… The love and warmth which emanate from this being to the dying person are utterly beyond words and he feels completely surrounded by it and taken up in it, completely at ease and (Continued next page).

G. Ask it what parts.

C. The heart. It actually gives the image of actually exposing the heart and when that happens this light comes in.

G. So it's showing you how to do that. Is that something you want?

(Since the client was fearful of going into the light, the guide checks his willingness for the light to go into him. The guide always respects the client's will).

C. Yeah. I can imagine that now. I see the heart exposed and it becomes bathed in the light from this source. This is the same light that heals and it's the same light that protects – that energizes everything.

G. Stay with that experience and include your experience of wanting that. What do you experience as that happens?

(Evoking the client's desire for the light helps to deepen the experience.)

C. I experience this opening so that there's a shift of my consciousness from my head to my heart – so that I can talk from my heart. It's a happy feeling because it's from that source – there's an honesty that's – the heart doesn't have all these defenses like the head so that by the time it comes out of the head it always goes through this tremendous distilling and distorting process. So that what comes out is never the truth – or it's almost always a distortion. Like there's a little factory there and men are lined up to mold the words to make sure that they're going to come out to protect the other person, to protect me, to protect everything. Whereas, when the heart speaks, it just comes out.

(He begins to analyze the experience rather than staying focused within it, so the guide brings him back to it.)

G. Stay with the experience of that light coming into your heart for a moment and get a sense for where you are in relationship to that source of light. How close you are. What's your position in the context of the dialogue you were having?

C. I have the image of being able to go right up to it and to experience not having to go in and merge with it. My heart is still there, still out as the light and warmth pour into it.

G. What about the intensity, the blinding quality?

C. It's not so intense that I have to look away – it's toned down a lot. I can now be more of a receptacle for it.

G. How did it tone down, how did that happen?

---

accepted in the presence of this being." pp. 58-59. The empirical evidence points to the fact that this is one of the deepest archetypes in the human unconscious which seems to be gradually and increasingly emerging into consciousness as part of the natural process of self-realization (actualization).

Counseling Case Study

C. I don't know if it's toned down or that I got used to it.

(After checking his experience, the guide made Joseph aware of the option to change his relationship to the light by merging with it now that he's experienced it as a healing and protecting energy. She directed him to tell the light what he wanted to both facilitate further dialogue and help him clarify his choice.)

C. It's no longer forcing me to look away.

G. Be aware of your relationship to it now – how close you are. See if that's the way you want it to be. Is there any way you want it to change or have it be different?

C. Just the image of - to take pieces of it with me so I can continue to have that inside of me.

G. Allow yourself to experience choosing that relationship.

(The guide deepened the experience of the client's will.)

C. I have the experience that this is everything that I want and it's life force… the same force that gets things done.

G. Tell that source what your choice is.

C. My choice is to bring it down into my physical body – here on earth now – using it in joy and sustenance and for my own physical well being – and it's a force to help me manifest all the qualities of goodness that I have potential for within me…. diffused that throughout my body – especially my heart.

G. Now, let it respond to what you said. Open yourself to hearing its response.

C. I am with you and I am in you. Take my power and go with that in peace.

G. How do you feel toward it?

C. Good toward it. A right balance - right relationship with it.

G. Stay with that right relationship with the light. Stay with what your heart says. See if there's a word that describes your feelings right now.

C. Grateful – gratitude.

G. Holding that experience of gratitude and with the light flowing into your heart, turn toward the earth now… what do you see as you do that?

(By having Joseph turn toward the earth at this point, the guide has brought him into relationship with it while he was still experiencing the light. In this way, he can get a better understanding of how the light relates to is earthly existence and a better understanding of how he can bring the light into his daily life.)

C. First, I think I saw… I focused on the ocean coming up on the shore… hospitable, receptive place.

G. From that same place in your heart, see if you can find the quality of feeling you have toward the earth.

C. My heart has a desire to connect – for attunement to it. A desire to reach out and connect to it … everything – water, elements, sand, people.

G. Stay in touch with both the experience of the gratitude toward the light – allowing it to flow into your heart and at the same time, the desire to connect to the earth and to people. Allow those two experiences to come into relationship. See how they come together.

C. Gratitude to the light for what it's given me – including strength, physical strength and energy and also strength that's required to be open and have that received – that I am able to make those connections and experience attunement.

G. Slowly bring the experience back with you into the room and open your eyes when you feel ready… If it seems to go away – go back inside for a moment and get it back. (long pause) See what connections you can make between what was happening when in relation to this source of light and that part that has the fear of the giant/destroyer – that's afraid of being too big – of not maintaining a low profile… how do they relate now?

C. There's no part of that giant/destroyer in that white light – that's a pure, powerful, benevolent source that's all – there's no such thing as illness, as destruction… there's only strength and power and energy – I don't think it has any connection to this giant/destroyer at all – whatever name you want to put on it. I can relate to that without any problem – that self or soul or God-force or whatever it is.

G. See if you can get a sense from what the part that's afraid of the destroyer thinks of this source.

C. It's not afraid of this source… it's not trying to stop the earth – to destroy or mutilate – in fact, just the opposite.

(The guide brought him back to the original issue to see differences that have occurred and help the client make them conscious. She asked Joseph if he saw any connection to this source & the ideal model of the sun filled thirty story building from the previous session.)

C. I want to be assured that I will survive – that it will survive – that the giant/destroyer won't knock it down. Now that I have the light, it's more real than the giant. It can help me build the structure… it's really true… I can let go of that fear.

She told him that the next step would be for him to include the experience of light in his life.

Counseling Case Study

After further discussion relating achievement to maintaining a low profile, Joseph realized that achievement doesn't necessarily lead to destruction. He thought about his total rejection of approval –seeking through ambition after the disease in this way, "I was viewing myself from a point where I saw all the things which preceded my illness and wanted to change (them) as if they were causative."

The guide had him articulate what the difference was in the quality of achievement that he now saw. He replied, "Two different things… here achievement is a by-product of what I'm doing."

After the session, Joseph wrote, "one of the more important distinctions that was made in the session was between the old achievement and the new achievement. In the old, I was hell-bent on achieving to get approval from father and father figures; if I did not achieve, then I suffered their disapproval and ultimately my own sever condemnation. I never want to condemn myself again (this is a way of killing myself.) And so I said the hell with achievement and the hell with approval. But I overreacted so that I did not want to do anything in which it might appear that I was trying to achieve. This attitude, to the extent that it is still operative, slows me down in the work I want to do. The attitude I prefer to maintain is that achievement would perhaps be a by-product of my efforts. I should not fear it; nor should I seek it…"

"I recall having the light go into my heart and expressing the desire to speak more from the heart… I was aware of it today in two instances: meeting a man at a pool, learning that he had a stomach problem and then teaching him autogenics, sharing my work and myself; speaking with my father on the phone – aware of an honest and open exchange."

"For the next days I would have images of the light at different times in the day. I noticed how aware I was of making an honest connection… My experience has been that I have had many more authentic exchanges with people."

Joseph was going through a natural process of the balancing and synthesis of opposites.* Before his illness, he was an over-achiever – totally identified with excellence in his accomplishments. In an effort to correct this compulsion afterwards, he over compensated and for several years acted out the opposite extreme. Having experienced both polarities, the natural process of growth would allow him a wider range of expression – the ability to consciously choose between the attitudes depending on his purpose for any particular task, and eventually to transcend the limitations of the polarity entirely.

However, in Joseph's case, the strong fear of the giant/destroyer concept was blocking the progress of this natural balancing. By helping Joseph work through his fears on the various levels where they affected his life, the natural process could unfold and be accelerated.

After his seventh session, Joseph wrote, "… I realized that a part of me still wants (as it once did long ago) to stand out, to make its mark, to distinguish itself… I am beginning to realize that without achievement, or without at least the desire to achieve, life can become less than exciting. I am owning my desire to achieve (but even as I say this, I want to have it a sanctified, purified, transformed into

---

*The Balancing and Synthesis of Opposites by Roberto Assagioli, M.D. Psychosynthesis Inst. P.R.R. Issue No. 29, p.4.

something noble.) And why not noble? Why must I think of my desire to stand out as something base? I keep thinking of something I read in Ken Wilbur's The Spectrum of Consciousness. In substance it was that we unnecessarily limit ourselves when we think in either-or terms. It doesn't have to be either this or that: it can be both this and that. (His underlining.)

When consulted on the important issue of achievement, Joseph's Wise Old Man advised:

"Don't suppress your desire to achieve – use it to achieve something of Value, something Good. If you desire fame in writing fiction, write a novel that contains Wisdom and Truth. Harness that part as you would a horse and let it gallop in the direction you choose."

He was very excited about this insight describing it as "using skillful will to execute something by Good Will."

During the next eight months, Joseph had two sessions which dealt with subpersonalities (not relevant to this case) and his wife had a prolonged illness that necessitated testing for the possibility of cancer (results were negative). Andrea's illness activated a "frightened, terrified part" of Joseph that had intense feelings of "fragility". He experienced a "fear of abandonment" as though Andrea were dying and consequently felt tremendously vulnerable. He dealt with this issue in his next two sessions.

Joseph was guided to experience these feelings, then allow an image of the experience to emerge. He saw a "raging baby" who was screaming. "That was the way I felt," he attested, "unable to function, real fragility."

(The guide's direction and strategy were to penetrate to the core need of this part through dialogue with the baby, so that Joseph could release related feelings and assume responsibility for meeting its needs in an acceptable way that was in line with his growth.)

At first, Joseph was ashamed and humiliated by the raging baby because it was so unmanly. He rejected it and simply wanted it to "shut up". The baby looked "premature, ugly, sickly, thin" and felt disgusted by it. (It's not unusual for a client to totally reject a part of himself that he has denied all his life. Often, that's the reason it was originally repressed – becomes it simply doesn't fit or is opposed to the client's self-concept.) The guide knew that it was important, however, to keep Joseph in dialogue with the rejected part – while acknowledging and expressing his feelings toward it in order to work toward acceptance of the fact that it is there and needs to be recognized, accepted and heard before a resolution could be reached. Acceptance frequently takes place spontaneously as the client begins to understand its true needs and motives.

As the dialogue continued, Joseph realized that the baby was raging because he was afraid of being alone because no one was coming to pick him up. He needed mother and she wasn't there. Joseph became more understanding. As he accepted the infant and shared these feelings with him, the image began to transform from a "raging little monster – so distorted and ugly" to becoming quiet, growing bigger and stronger until he could stand up by himself. (Transformations frequently occur once an image is heard rather than habitually being denied expression.)

Counseling Case Study

The guide helped Joseph uncover the child's need to be loved totally. He wanted complete acceptance and to know that – no matter what – he wouldn't be left alone.

Joseph agreed to love him and took him inside himself – into his heart. He then experienced himself as fearless, secure, feeling warmth, solidity and self-love. He had a sense of completion.

Bringing the client back to the original issue involving Andrea, the guide suggested that Joseph speak to his Wise Man about her. The Wise Man assured him that as he loved and took care of this child-part inside himself, it would be less dependent on Andrea to fill his needs, and he would love her more solidly.

For homework, the guide suggested that Joseph check in on the baby often and dialogue with him. Joseph agreed to assume responsibility for giving this infant part of himself the love and total acceptance that he needed.

Self nurturance is an important aspect of coordinating the child within. As the client gives him love, he'll start to grow and eventually become mature enough to become integrated with the core personality. This process gives the client access to all the good, positive qualities of the child-like sensitivity, playfulness, sense of wonder, etc. that are often repressed along with negative aspects of child subpersonalities. By transforming negative into positive attributes, consciously evoking and building desirable qualities, a client is able to transform his personality into a vehicle that is responsive to his Higher Self.*

Ten months and seven sessions after beginning counseling, Joseph was using his mind to allow his feelings in the moment. The following dramatic example showed how he was able to "ground" the work and bring it into his life.

"My wife's illness, especially when she was initially very ill, produced a lot of anxiety/fear and even some anger…I was really frightened that she might die… there was a part of me that was a ball of anxiety and fear in the early mornings… I used the exercise of disidentification and also the skillful will to shift away from experiencing that part… It was an extraordinary experience to be able to observe the shift from this ball of anxiety to someone who was calm and confident… I did this by first choosing not to be that ball anxiety. Then I used the following affirmation: 'I choose to know Andrea is well.' I said it over and over until I experienced that knowing and then, I was calm and confident. In the following days I would shift back and forth between these two experiences.

"I have known about the Fragile Part of me for some time. If I sleep late, until nine to ten A.M., it seems I am insulated from experiencing it. However, if I get up early and there's any cause for anxiety, then I am apt to experience the Fragile Part. I think the Fragile Part is terrified of being left alone or

---

*The principles and practice of transmutation of psychological energies are described extensively by Assagioli, Psychosynthesis, A Manual of Principles and Techniques, Viking Press, New York, 1971, pp. 267-277, & by Crampton, "Psychological Energies & Transformations, " Synthesis Graduate School, San Francisco, (ed.)

abandoned. I was most in touch with it when I left the emergency room on Thursday. The tears began to flow and then the automatic blocking mechanism I have shut off the pain/sadness. But I was able to be my own therapist and say: 'It's OK. Allow that. It's alright to allow that.' And the sadness and fear poured out."

At this point, Joseph was becoming more in control of his personality – making clear choices about how he wanted to be, and then, carrying them through. "I am much more aware of the choice I have in producing my own mood," he wrote. "When I was running every minute of the day, I often noticed like a muttering – a voice that was beginning to express self-pity. I was able to not have myself shift into that feeling of self-pity before it came on me, by simply choosing to remain in good spirits and saying to the self-pity voice, 'I don't want to feel badly. Yes, it's tough, but too bad.'"

The difference between allowing feelings of pain and sadness to pour out over his wife and not allowing himself to become identified with a self-pity voice, illustrate an important point. The idea is not to simply allow unrestricted expression of feelings indiscriminately. Rather, integrating the personality gives a person the freedom to discriminate between conflicting feelings (at any one moment there can be two or more different feelings present), choosing which one – if any – he wishes to allow, regulating its intensity and deciding when to shut it off. The personality integrating around the "I" is in control of every personality aspect and activates or inhibits each at will. The threat of losing Andrea triggered a deeper layer of Joseph's fear of abandonment, and he reported feelings of fragility again in his next session. He experienced it as a "fear of the loss of love and I felt underneath that was a 'root fear of abandonment and a feeling of being manipulated by my mother.'"

The guide helped him separate these feelings from a "tremendous amount of anger toward my mother" (that had been triggered by anger at his female guide when she cancelled a session). He connected it to an incident that had occurred at age eleven or twelve when he had stabbed his mother's car seat and ruined it in a fit of rage. This was totally out of character for Joseph, who was a "good kid" who never expressed anger.

He recalled a pre-school nursery story about "sons protecting their mothers from the dragon, from the ogre – it's damn clear, from my father; I accepted that – I was raised a defender – that's my 100% loyalty."

The guide hypothesized that Joseph had made a bond of loyalty to his mother as a young child that carried a great price. She decided to help him look at the content and meaning of the bond and help him release the feelings that were holding the outdated pattern in place.

G. What's the price you paid for that?

C. It distorted my relationship with my father – that's one thing. I was raised to consider my father an antagonist, with a build-in bias that I was going to be on my mother's side. The other part was that I had to be like my mother, because she was good and he was bad.

Counseling Case Study

The guide asked Joseph to make a statement to his mother about their relationship and to experience the feelings that accompanied that. He felt tears and sadness around feelings of being 100% loyal to his mother. Identified as the little boy within, he told mother:

C. I'll protect you against him. That was the bargain. If you protect me, I'll always protect you. I'll stay 100% loyal to you – I promise that I'll protect you against him. He's no good.

G. What are you experiencing?

C. Anger at my father. I'll fight him if I have to. I'll kill him if I have to.

(Joseph started to beat rhythmically with his fist on the couch).

C. I can beat daddy. I can beat daddy.

G. Again.

C. He's only three. He doesn't have the strength. I can do it.

G. See your father.

She brought him into direct relationship with him in imagery in order to intensify the feelings.

C. He wants to come close to kiss me. His face is rough. "Keep away." I'm pushing him away. "Go away, go, go, go."

Under the guide's direction, Joseph told his father about his commitment to his mother.

C. I'm 100% loyal to mother. You're no good. I have to protect her from you. You're no good. You hurt her, scream at her. I'm taking care of her. She's mine. She's my mother. She hates you and I hate you. Leave us alone. Get out – go away. (Shouting) THIS IS US – HER AND ME – GET OUT!

After father left, the child felt good because the threat was gone. He told mother, "There's nothing to be afraid of when he's gone. I love you. Don't love him." But mother looked unhappy and Joseph felt afraid. The guide penetrated this moment of fear.*

The little boy asked mother, "Did I do something (wrong)? I got him out… I did what you told me to do…

---

*This is important because it can easily be missed. In fact, the more painful or fearful an event, the quicker the client will unconsciously pass over it in an effort to keep it repressed.

The normal pattern is to experience and assimilate. Initial trauma arises when things move too fast to be assimilated. This is complicated by a child's inability to correctly perceive things that are going on in the adult world – so that distortions result from the combination of these factors. The basic technique is to slow things down, expand the moment and see what really happened, give the client space to re-experience the various feelings connected with the event and then, go through it again to get mental understanding and the meaning of the event in order to restore the natural growth process & assimilate the experience.

I thought that'd make you happy…when you're not happy, it makes me feel frightened."

G. Allow the fear.

C. It makes me feel wrong, vulnerable. I can be attacked. I'm unprotected. Something's missing, like a whole layer of skin, like all my nerves are exposed.

G. How did that happen, that suddenly you became afraid and vulnerable?

C. She didn't look happy, she looked sad.

G. What about that makes you afraid?

C. If she's sad because he leaves, maybe she doesn't want to protect me first – maybe she wants him.

G. Go back to the fear. Let yourself get what's wrong. What are you afraid of?

C. I don't trust her. If she's sad when he leaves, she may not protect me against him. I'll be finished, dead – he'll kill me.

G. Tell her you don't trust her.

C. I'm afraid you'll be loyal to him. What will I do if you're loyal to him after I've screamed and yelled at him? He'll come back and get me. He'll kill me. He'll put me in the cellar.

The guide evoked his anger at her betrayal.

C. I would be 100% loyal to you against him and you were supposed to be 100% loyal to me. Now you're not being that way. I don't like that. You have to protect me. I want 100%!

G. What do you experience as you say that?

C. A sense of righteousness. This is my right. I expect this – you're mine.

(Joseph felt a sense of power as he continued.)

C. Don't desert me – don't side with him ever. You have to be here all the time for me. Don't turn away from me… I want to control you. You can stop me from being frightened. I'm insisting on it! I DEMAND IT – YOU'RE MINE TO DEMAND TO BE THERE. I know how to hurt you badly. I'm powerful. I can scream and yell and say mean things. I know how to hurt you – that's what power is – to hurt.

G. See if you can get to the core of what you're angry about.

C. She won't give up her allegiance to him completely.

(When she wanted the father, too, this left him feeling like he was out on a limb).

C. I can't be loyal to you and I can't be loyal to him… I'm in a bind. I can't get out. I have to pretend I'm loyal to you and to him.

(The guide built the experience of the double bind as if it were happening in the moment. He experienced feeling alone… "fear that he'll get me – she won't protect me.")

G. What's that feel like, to be in that bind where you pushed him away and will never know when he'll come back… And you made a deal with her but she didn't keep it. What's the experience?

C. Always being afraid… always being anxious.

G. Allow some of the anxiety, allow some of that fear.

C. I feel tense, tight, scared – always scared. I don't know why, it's always there. It's the threat. It's always possible that he can come in.

G. What do you experience?

C. Pulling in.

G. Allow yourself to pull in.

C. I have to protect myself – to put a shell around me. Something to protect me from the fear – to insulate me.

It became dark, constraining, hard and uncomfortable. After awhile, everything's pulled in and constricted. He felt "cut off, trapped… I don't like it now that I put myself inside."

G. What do you need to get out?

C. The shell is thick, thicker than I wanted to make it. Crack the shell, get out of the shell, crawl…

G. Look around and see if there's any way out – any opening.

C. In the back I see light.

G. Move toward the light. Be in touch with your experience as you do that.

The guide encouraged Joseph to experience the intense feelings associated with the bind so that he could move through the block of fear to the other side. She recognized these feelings as classic symptoms of a birth experience that many clients relive when moving through patches of fear. In Joseph's case, they naturally unfolded to allow him to re-experience the feelings around his birth.

The original manner in which Joseph reacted to his experience of birth established the pattern for the way that he would relate to all future fearful experiences. Therefore, when we saw his father as a threat to his life (because of his exclusive love for his mother), the event activated this intrauterine fear pattern causing intense anxiety and fragility.

By consciously allowing the feelings as he moved through the experiences, he deactivated their charge.

C. Toward the light – there's more light.

G. What do you experience as you see more light?

C. My body's moving out, not so restricted. I can relax. I'll be alright as I move toward the light. It's longer than I thought it was.

G. Just keep moving toward the light. How far are you from the light now?

C. It's like a tunnel now – 20 or 30 feet away. I crawl through the tunnel – get out – pressing.

G. What's pressing?

C. I don't know.

G. Just allow it to press. Stay with your experience as fully as you can. Just go with it – even if you don't understand it. Something's pressing. Let it press. Keep moving toward the light.

C. It's easier now. It's getting closer.

G. Is there anything that you want to say to the light as you move closer to it?

C. I'm coming. I'm coming out. Not too bright, soft. I wanna come out, I wanna come out. I gotta get out.

G. What do you need to get out?

C. Push out, out (deep breathing).

G. Good, good. Stay in touch with really wanting to get to the light.

C. Gotta get out to the light … still dark (deep breathing, panting, long exhalations). I'm breathing!

G. (Long pause). Let yourself breathe.

Staying in touch with the desire to get out to the light eases and accelerates the process by aligning the client's desire with his goal. Dialoguing with the light also facilitates this and frequently the light's response will motivate the client to keep moving forward.

C. It's so nice to breathe. I feel like I've never breathed before. (continues to breathe deeply).

G. Just let yourself experience it fully. What's it like to be breathing and in the light?

C. It's good to be here.

G. What's your experience of being out.

C. Fresh, clean, grateful. My whole body's breathing.

Joseph felt cold. The guide told him to let in the warmth of the light. He experienced himself feeling warm, lying in a bassinette in the sunlight. Then he experienced love and satisfaction as his mother held him in her arms. The guide told him to bring the qualities of freshness, gratitude and love back with him to the room and open his eyes.

After discussing the Oedipal pattern (of desiring exclusive possession of mother and fear of being killed by father), the guide told Joseph to think about the experience of a three-year-old boy being afraid that his father will kill him and how that pattern affected his life and the price that he paid.

Afterwards, Joseph wrote, "The major insight from the Oedipal session…connects why my father work was so difficult. (This pattern) made me a helluva lot more afraid of my father. That seems the biggest price, the fear, the over-sensitivity to my father's demands… I've been afraid, have always been afraid that he might kill me. No wonder I never wanted to disappoint him, always wanted to please him… (This is) the source of (my) strong need for approval from authority figures… I wanted to cover up my 'crime.' And the root cause is my relationship with my mother… I became like mother; over protective, tendency to worry, a hypochondriac, a heaviness of being in the world. I no longer need to be like her to get her protection or to appease him to avoid his rejection and his wrath… I'm moving toward loyalty to myself, independence, freedom and power."

The session immediately following, dealt with understanding how the Oedipal pattern affected Joseph's life and grounding the new pattern of freedom that was emerging.

Joseph experienced "lightness and joy" as he anticipated freeing himself from this old pattern and felt that he was "no longer culpable in some way." He sensed a "freeing up of energy".

G. Allow the experience and describe it as you do.

C. Having more power, more energy. A certain tension that builds – like a spring coiling – I pull into myself, which can then release where I want it to go.

G. Experience that pulling… What is it you're pulling?

C. Me. That I'm compacting what's essentially me. It's a more purified experience – with nothing else getting in the way.

G. Where were you before?

C. Scattered, mixed with other's expectations – father, mother, strings, expectations, etc.

G. What allowed you to get yourself back?

C. Going back to untie improper connectedness to father and mother. Being able to see it, experience it and see the connection to what's happening today.

G. Can you see how this relates to freeing your will? How much freedom did you have regarding your father and authority figures?

C. Little or none. Fear and anxiety were controlling me.

G. Part of what you're doing is freeing your will from one of the places where it was trapped. That thing you put out is your will.

C. Right. I choose, I control it… I want to bring the freedom and energy totally to writing and counseling and I want to be completely free from emotional recriminations. There's so much I can bring to writing fiction that I learned here – so many techniques from Psychosynthesis. From Superconscious energy to becoming them, to having the Wise Old Man – so much richness.

Under the guide's direction, Joseph envisioned himself as he could be in the future as the sense of freedom and joy became more and more available. The essential quality of this "ideal model" was joy. She had him dialogue with this model and then, become it.

As the future Joseph, he experienced himself as the wise Patriarch. "I have the knowledge of the complexities of myself, I have mastered that in a functional way. And I can do so much with other people. Having taken apart and put together one engine, I can do that with other types of engines –the principles are the same."

G. See if you can get what you want to express as this being.

C. Freedom certainly. Their birthright is freedom but they experience the opposite. Freedom can be theirs- that's a fact. There are ways, steps, techniques, strategies to experience that, to make it a reality. And to be able to articulate the steps of how to get there as a teacher.

G. Is there anything else that seems important as this wiser, older person?

(Asking the client if there's anything else is very valuable because it gives him an opportunity to verbalize feelings or thoughts that are important for him but that the guide did not cover.)

C. I still have questions about my connection to my soul… I want to connect to it, because the intensity of the way I express myself will be determined by that connection.

Upon exploration, the guide found out that Joseph still feared the existence of a "father/God" and he was afraid that it might "kill me, knock me out of existence… similar to what the 3 year old felt his father would do to him – so there's the connection."

Here the fear that his father would kill him, which has been projected onto God, surfaces as the resistance to achieving the ideal model that he envisioned.

C. This whole thing about illness and feeling that I was at the mercy of that God and he came damn close to killing me. And part of my strategy has been to lie low – not address him, to eliminate him, to deny His existence... All those associations at age 3 stand in the way of ever wanting to acknowledge that he's my soul.

The guide, at this point, had Joseph express these feelings to his soul.

C. I'm afraid of you because of what you almost did to me – of killing me because I was bad. I'd just as soon kill you with my bare hands than you kill me.

This is the same pattern contained in the fantasy of killing the Deity and it recurs in later work.

The guide knew that Joseph had to cathart his anger toward God/father in order to release the repressed negative energy that still held the pattern in place. Therefore, she directed him to physically pound pillows to express his rage while he shouted to God (then to his own father, since one is a projection of the other), "I'm not going to let you kill me" over and over.

When the energy was spent, Joseph's body felt cleaned out and powerful. He imagined his father and stated to him:

C. "Your negative influence over me is ended. Your ability to tug and pull on me is over. I reach out to you from gratitude, love and appreciation for the good that you've done in my life and not out of fear, anger or resentment. I've severed my connection to you. I'll continue to make that separation stronger and stronger and always be available to act from my heart... adult... free."

The guide then asked Joseph to reach up to his soul and describe his experience.

C. Some sense of reservoir, source, creative love that's what made the Universe and I'm connected to that – whatever it is. The sense is impersonal, benign. I don't get threatened by it. I can relate to it on that level.

G. Does it seem any different now than it did?

C. It's non-personal, non-God. If I keep it in that perspective, there's nothing negative between it and me. I'm not concerned with denying its existence – it can just be there. I always thought about God's justice – retribution.

G. What's your experience of that?

C. The soul has none of those qualities. I have to let go of all the garbage I was raised with and part of that is my relationship to my father.

In the after discussion, the guide told Joseph that more anger might come up and to simply release it by pounding pillows again if it did. She also asked him to write about the fear.

When referring to "cleaning up the father principle," he wrote: "Look at my progression: 1) I'm afraid you'll kill me, 2) I'm not going to let you kill me, 3) I want to know you (not the father yet, but the Self)… my fear comes from the child's fear of the father."

In the Oedipal session, Joseph expressed pain over his exclusive loyalty to mother, anger toward her for breaking her bargain, and fear of father killing him. In the next session, he was able to cathart anger toward God/father. Both sessions worked on the same Oedipal dynamic, but each released different repressed feelings. One laid the groundwork for the other and allowed it to go to a deeper level; i.e. go beyond the fear of father and express anger to him (in imagery) for having threatened his life. By repressing the anger and harmlessly directing it onto pillows (through pounding) Joseph allowed it to transform into personal power which he then used to assert his human rights and essential dignity. This is another aspect of Joseph's newly- emerging pattern of personal freedom.

An even deeper level of the fear of being abandoned was below the Oedipal fear. The "raging baby" represented Joseph's fear of Andrea abandoning him.* The Oedipal session uncovered fear of mother abandoning him to father's wrath. These were outer layers of the core pattern (or co-ex) that seemed to have its roots buried in Joseph's past incarnation history. (Joseph had no previous belief in the possibility of past incarnations and remained incredulous afterwards. It is not necessary for either client or guide to accept the possibility of past incarnations as fact. Valuable therapeutic work can be done very effectively if one or both think of unconscious images that emerge (which seem to be related to past lives) as symbols that contain the dysfunctional patterns that need to be changed. Working at this level of unconscious memory has proved beneficial to client growth.**

Three months passed between the "raging baby" session and Joseph's final two sessions dealing with images of previous incarnations that manifested the recurring patterns relating to abandonment in Joseph's present life.

While working with a new guide, in the next to last session, a similar image of a screaming baby emerged. The guide wondered if the fear of abandonment was the result of Joseph feeling like he had abandoned himself, and then projected the abandonment onto his parents (thinking they were abandoning him).

---

*It was important that Joseph recognize, accept and assume responsibility for caring for this infant part of himself because selflove and self-nurturance – though an essential practice of good psychological hygiene – have been neglected in Western culture.

**Many notable researchers such as Stevenson and Grof accept past incarnations as a plausible and valuable hypothesis. The reader is referred below for additional reading on the subject.

S. Grof, M.D. , Realms of the Human Unconscious, Observations from LSD Research, E.P. Dutton, New York, 1976, pp. 173-176, 206.

I. Stevenson: Cases of the Reincarnational Type. Vol 1.Ten Cases in India, University Press of Virginia, Charlottesville, 1975.Ibid. Vol. 2. Ten Cases in Sri Lanka, Univ. Press of Virginia, Charlottesville, 1977. Ibid. Vol. 3 Fifteen Cases in Thailand, Lebanon, and Turkey, University Press of Virginia, Charlottesville, 1978.

Counseling Case Study

Joseph's presenting issue was a feeling of abandonment when his previous guide resigned from the counseling center and had forgotten to cancel a scheduled session with him. When he arrived, she wasn't there. This made him angry. The new guide evoked these angry feelings and directed Joseph to physically pound pillows to cathart his anger toward the previous one. As he pounded, he began to see different targets – most especially his father. So he told his father as he released his anger, "Go, go, I wanna be free. It has to do with who I am. I am good. I don't have to prove it." When finished, Joseph felt contentment. The guide had him describe and experience the contentment and the goodness, and took him back to the first time he experienced that goodness. He imagined himself as a quiet, content baby in his crib. His parents came in. Father played with him and mother nursed him. All was well. But when mother put him down and left with father, the baby became angry and started screaming and raging to bring her back.

In order to see more clearly what was happening inside the infant, the guide told Joseph to get a sense of what the baby would really like to do – if he had the power. Joseph saw the baby pull his parents back into the room by their necks with a magical cord – until she picked him up again. The guide asked what the baby wanted to do now. The baby tied the father in the corner and said to him, "You son of a bitch; I'm in charge here and went back to nursing.

(The guide thought that this was a strange attitude for a baby to take toward a father who had just been playing with him. So, she asked Joseph what effect tying father up in a corner had on the contentment of nursing. He replied that it gave him pleasure to keep father tied up. The guide brought Joseph into direct dialogue by having him tell father how much he was enjoying this. He told father that he felt "damn good" about it- now he can't take his mother away from him.

The father's voice sounded like a "whip" to the baby, so he put a gag on him and preceded to smile while he "kicked him in the ass." The guide asked what father was feeling. The baby answered, "humiliation…so I do it more." Then Joseph said, "That's the exact same feeling I get when my mother and I beat him at cards in present time!"

When asked why he was treating his father this way, he said, "He deserves it," and told the story about father slapping him in the face and threatening him at age 13, making him feel humiliated and angry. The guide had Joseph imagine himself at that time and stand up to father to demand respect for himself as a person. He saw that the threat disappeared when he stood up for himself and without fear, Joseph connected with his own goodness.

Joseph saw the pattern. When he felt powerless in relation to father, he lost touch with his own sense of goodness and felt disconnected. Hatred and revenge followed.

She had him reconnect to his desire to humiliate and kick his father and asked if he experienced his own goodness then. He said no. Instead, he experienced "meanness… badness, mankind avenging himself on someone else… out of that…people got burned at the stake." The guide asked him to image a scene where someone was being "burned at the stake."* Joseph saw a "Christ-like figure… tied up to a cross and being burned at the same time… and a group of people standing around gleeful, saying he deserved it… he's a terrible trouble maker… anything's justified… people are whipping him… a sense of justification and rightness about it." She asked him if the pleasure was also there. "Yeah, because you did it to me, now I'm doing it to you – revenge."

He described himself as one of the soldiers who are getting pleasure out of beating the "criminal" with a whip. Joseph cried as he witnessed this scene and said, "My tears are saying, 'I'm sorry' for inflicting pain on another human being." As he said this, he got more in touch with own goodness. Then, he looked into the dying man's eyes and sensed love and forgiveness coming from him. Joseph then said, "I'm the only one standing in the way of my own forgiveness… he forgives me.*

After experiencing forgiveness, Joseph felt "good, cleansed… contrite… humble… appreciative." He determined to use his power in a right way. The guide asked him to imagine using his will to inhibit the desire to humiliate for pleasure and when he did this, he connected once again to a sense of his own goodness.

The guide pointed to the pattern in the discussion after the experience: when he didn't stand up for himself, he disconnected from his own sense of goodness, felt powerless and wanted revenge. On the other hand, when he did demand respect for himself, he stayed connected to his goodness and the desire to humiliate for pleasure wasn't there.

For homework, he agreed to look for situations where he experienced this urge to find subtle ways of humiliating people with whom he was not being straight, for times when he covered over that urge to humiliate by being differential. Neither action uses his power rightly. He was also to practice asserting himself rather than buying into his feelings of powerlessness and abandoning his own sense of goodness. (This is an example of replacing an old pattern with a new and better one.)

Joseph wrote the following statements after this session: "Watch for the two sides of acting: 1) teasing, humiliating father, brother, because I don't stand up to them; 2) being too deferential towards them and authority figures. Latter likely to lead to resentment, feelings of powerlessness.

IF I STAND UP TO HIM AND DEMAND RESPECT, 'I DON'T NEED TO HUMILIATE HIM'. Also, as I stand up to him, I experience power and freedom and therefore, I don't need to treat him badly.

As I reflect upon it, this is a very important connection. With my going back home, I can anticipate pulls from father and brother as well as others. I need to make clear in a strong but gentle way who I am. I also need to do this with all authority figures. Standing up for who I am is a form of owning my power and creates maximum freedom, so that I can choose to do what I perceive as my work: manifesting Superconscious qualities in writing and counseling.

Message I got from Christ figure was that I should not misuse power in the future. Felt much better after the experience, having unburdened myself. Saw the connection that misusing power takes away my sense of goodness."

---

*The guide regressed the client into past life using the phrase of "being burned at the stake." She also could have used the phrase of the father's voice being, "like a whip," since powerful words like this are often past life clues.

Counseling Case Study

Joseph now earned an M.A. in Psychology and was planning to return to Chicago to practice.

Joseph's final session began with the question: "What was it like to rest in your goodness?" He replied: "A good experience – I felt centered, in control – in fact, it may have allowed what I consider a turning point in my life to happen! I have always wanted to perform as a stand-up comic using a different kind of humor to lift people by making them laugh at the human condition – to rid them of misconceptions about God, for example not using humor to put myself or anybody else down – the way our culture presently uses it."

He told of how he had recently taken advantage of an opportunity to perform as a comic for the public. He had to wait five hours for his turn at entertaining people in a nightclub. "Part of me was terrified, " he said, and "wanted to flee."

He dis-identified, "drew on everything I learned… reduced the fear, brought in will, mediated the whole day on courage… I had to feel good about myself to do it… I meditated on the transpersonal quality of humor… of making my personality a vehicle… I even dialogued with my Soul." The guide asked what was its response. The message was, "You can do this… assurance came into me, knowing was amplified… realizing God's not those false images." The guide asked, "What is it?" "It's guiding me, I can trust it… it's out for best interests in the broadest sense … it'll tell me in crisis. 'This is what you need to do.' I had that happen before – a revelation."

When the guide asked how this was a turning point in his life, Joseph said, "I was able to act beyond what I thought were my capabilities… (I) used everything to go beyond – stretching … letting go of personality incriminations … of worrying about the outcome… (I got) in line with my centered choice."

He went on to say that he had a sense that he'll be talking before groups in the future and this was good practice for using humor with them.

"My body was rebelling… I was soothing and dialoguing with it" …he told it that he was not going to be "murdered or slain or crucified" at a "primitive, physical level." Part of him felt he was "in danger" – that it would be "ridiculed and condemned."

The guide asked what was different in this experience. He replied that before he "couldn't act because of fear," after, he had acted even with the fear. It "significantly increased trust in myself and trust in my Soul and the Universe." (This was a very big step for Joseph – to act for something he believed in before a large group of people – in spite of the danger/fear of mass disapproval. He said he didn't care if they laughed at him or not. He had watched them put down other comedians – had gotten himself pretty clean from that expectation. The guide directed him to imagine that his Soul had feelings and asked him how it felt when he acted beyond his fear to express something good. It felt "joy, applause, celebration, encouragement – all with a lot of energy in back of them." It was celebrating "this thing we've done together." it told him to "continue on his new level." He said he felt like he grounded a good part of the book, The Act of Will. Joseph said, "I like the approval... it's a paradox because it's my approval – I like getting my approval." He felt "lightness like he was "carrying less baggage."

The guide asked if he'd like to work on the fear that he dis-identified from to get more clarity and control of it. He consented and she asked him to get back in touch with the feelings that he experienced when he felt like he'd "be crucified." He allowed an image to emerge for these feelings and he saw himself as an old, frail Christian missionary ministering to black natives. But the natives in power were scaring the rest by making them think that the priest was evil. He saw himself as having already been beaten with broken bones and about to be killed by them. They tied him to a post, ridiculed, taunted and slapped and harassed him as they feasted and enjoying pricking his skin with branches.

At first, Joseph witnessed the scenes in the imagery as an observer. Then, the guide deepened the experience by having him become the priest and go through it all again.

As an old man, hanging all day in the hot sun, he felt exhausted and was mortified that they were desecrating his body. As the missionary, Joseph wondered where God was and why he hadn't helped. He began to doubt that there was a God as the natives laughed at him and taunted him about his God. His doubts said there was no God – though another part of him knew there was.

In order to express his feelings, the guide had him stay with the doubting part and tell God how he felt.

> C. You placed me in a position where I don't know anything. Why have you done that to me? I feel angry. STOP THIS NOW. I want to tell him to let them kill me now. It's terrible. There's nothing to do but hang.

> G. How do you feel about God?

> C. I want to give up on you.

> G. Are you giving up on him?

> C. Yeah. I just want to be disconnected from him. If he's there, he's there. If not, he's not. I just want peace. As long as I wonder, I don't have peace.

> (Joseph continued and said that it was just a question of time and he was getting numb.)

> G. Go back to before the numbness... to when you were angry. From here, what do you want to do to God?

> C. I want to shake my fist, plead. I don't have enough strength to protest.

> G. Protest verbally.

> C. I've given my life to serve you. Now, it's being taken from me. The least you can do is make it happen quickly.

> G. Tell him how you feel.

C. I'm angry that you're not doing it that way. Disappointed.

(He feebly expressed hate, but a "part underneath knows that's not real."

G. Stay with the hate in the moment. What would it have you do?

C. Renounce and condemn God. Anything to save myself. I know that's not possible.
He then tells God:

C. I would do it if I could, I would save myself first.

G. How do you feel?

C. Mixed. I feel that that's right. Another part knows that's not an option, there's no reason to hate.

This part then, turned away from God (abandoned Him); he put a barrier between himself and God. As soon a he did this, Joseph verbalized the futility of the attempt by saying, "You can't separate yourself from this source." The guide told him to let himself die and go beyond. He looked down at his dead body as he moved toward the light. The guide asked him to look at the old man's whole life to see what had been useful that he wanted to take with him. He said of the old man, "He remained steadfast, attached to his purpose, loving."

G. From here, as the soul/High Self, what's important in the moment when the priest turned back to you?

C. A connection remained. There's a distinction between the part that turned and a part that didn't. The part that turned is an illusion. It was his personality's response to pain.

G. How do you feel toward him?

C. Compassion, appreciation, loving, connected to him.

The guide told him to move toward a place of rest and he experienced "joy, peace – no thoughts or words, no name, just like being the center of a smile. I am the smile…radiance." She told Joseph to stay connected to the radiance, peace and joy, to come back into his body and open his eyes.

As a missionary, Joseph experienced humiliation at the hands of the natives that he came to help, while as a soldier, he was the one who was humiliating the dying Christ-figure. Both sides of this pattern were being continued in this life.

Joseph recalled experiences as a child where he felt humiliated by father and hated him for doing it. And, Joseph also found subtle ways to humiliate his father (like beating him at cards) which he enjoyed.

He had assumed that God hated him for inflicting pain on another human being while a soldier and that he was being punished for being bad as the old priest. (In one of his write-ups after a session, Joseph had said that God had tried to kill him through disease "because I was bad.")

Joseph wrote about the pattern set in the missionary life, "God is my protector. He is good. I love Him and am 100% loyal to him. But when he abandoned me, (He didn't protect me) I got killed by natives because they hated me for loving and serving God." He then got angry at God and hated him. The correlate in this life which repeated itself at age three would be: Mother is my protector. She is good. I love her and am 100% loyal to her. But she abandoned me to the threat of being killed by my father, who hates me for loving and being 100% loyal to my mother. He then became angry at mother and hated father for threatening his life. Unconsciously, Joseph lived in fear that father would kill him which caused chronic anxiety easily activated by circumstances.

The reaction formation to this pattern was an attempt to please and appease father and win his approval at all costs because it was mortally dangerous to incur father's wrath. He acted this out by abandoning two scholarships earned through academic achievement even though he had chosen psychology as his life's work in order to appease father by becoming an engineer and going into the family business.

As the dying missionary, Joseph expressed feelings of hate toward God for allowing him to die in that way. This pattern would repeat itself through Joseph's present hatred of father. This, of course, was repressed because Joseph feared that if father realized it, he would kill him.

The son then, turned his hatred of the father inward onto himself as his wish to destroy himself. (Note: Images of self destruction that he spoke of in the beginning). These feelings (he now believes) caused the disease which almost killed him.

The abandonment pattern acted as a filter through which Joseph viewed his life experience. Because of his previous incarnation experience of having believed that God hated and abandoned him, Joseph interpreted being stricken with leukemia as God's deliberate attempt to kill him. Since he believed he had survived through his own efforts and will to live, he felt that he needed to hide his existence from God to avoid divine wrath. (Same pattern as with father). Therefore, he again over compensated by repressing all desire for achievement – because achievement would make him stand out and God might notice that he was still alive and strike him down again.

In terms of future work, Joseph had a big breakthrough in the last few sessions. A lot got moved, changed, readjusted in his process. The next step would be to complete unfinished pieces, clean up mental distortions by going back into these two past lives, going through them again slowly (one at a time, of course) releasing residual emotional energy and cleaning up any misconceptions. In this way, the guide would help make the new patterns that emerged solid and help Joseph see how they apply to everyday life (ground them). At that point, it would become clear what to do next.

In conclusion, the following are statements that Joseph wrote upon termination of counseling:

Counseling Case Study

"Over the past two years, I have emerged in several ways and I believe that pyschosynthesis, and particularly my didactic counseling has had a significant part in helping me make those changes. I believe my heart is more open; I have greater access to my feelings – I am more conscious of my feelings than I have ever been – aware when they're present, aware when they're not and perhaps should be; I have greater confidence in my intuitive and abstract mind; I am more my own person, much less subject to influence by approval seeking needs; I am more conscious of what I perceive to be my life work – I now have well defined goals for the near future. I am more conscious of myself as a willing person and am able to use the skillful will to better accomplish what I chose. Over the past two years, my emotional "belief" in the existence of a father/God has diminished; intellectually, I long ago stopped believing in that form of divinity. My hope, and at times belief, is that I am part of what is immortal and divine, part of the creator and the created – a Soul."